Astral Mysticism & Otherworldly Music

Celestial Hymns from Qumran to the Odes of Solomon That May Be "Extraterrestrial"

A Modern Translation

Adapted for the Contemporary Reader

Various Ancient Writers

Translated by Tim Zengerink

© **Copyright 2025**
All rights reserved.

It is not legal to reproduce, duplicate, or transmit any part of this document in either electronic means or in printed format. Recording of this publication is strictly prohibited and any storage of this document is not allowed unless with written permission from the publisher except for the use of brief quotations in a book review.

This book contains works of fiction. Any resemblance to persons living or dead, or places, events, or locations is purely coincidental.

Table of Contents

Preface - Message to the Reader 1

Introduction 5

Odes of Solomon 12

    Ode 1 13
    Ode 2 13
    Ode 3 13
    Ode 4 14
    Ode 5 16
    Ode 6 17
    Ode 7 18
    Ode 8 21
    Ode 9 23
    Ode 10 24
    Ode 11 24
    Ode 12 27
    Ode 13 28
    Ode 14 28
    Ode 15 29
    Ode 16 30
    Ode 17 32
    Ode 18 33
    Ode 19 35
    Ode 20 36
    Ode 21 37

Ode 22 38
Ode 23 39
Ode 24 41
Ode 25 42
Ode 26 43
Ode 27 44
Ode 28 45
Ode 29 46
Ode 30 47
Ode 31 48
Ode 32 49
Ode 33 50
Ode 34 51
Ode 35 51
Ode 36 52
Ode 38 53
Ode 39 55
Ode 40 56
Ode 41 57
Ode 42 59

Thunder: Perfect Mind 61

Thank You for Reading 72

Preface - Message to the Reader

What If You Could Help Rebuild the Greatest Library in Human History?

Thousands of years ago, the Library of Alexandria stood as the crown jewel of human achievement — a sanctuary where the collected wisdom of every known civilization was gathered, preserved, and shared freely.

And then, it was lost.

Through fire, conquest, and the slow erosion of time, humanity lost not just books — but ideas, dreams, discoveries, and stories that could have changed the world forever.

Today, the Library of Alexandria lives again — and you are invited to be a part of its restoration.

Our mission is simple yet profound:

To rebuild the greatest library the world has ever known, and to translate all timeless works into every language and dialect, so that no seeker of knowledge is ever left behind again.

By joining our movement to rebuild the modern Library of Alexandria, you become part of an unprecedented mission:

- **Unlimited Access to the Greatest Audiobooks & eBooks Ever Written:**

  Instantly explore thousands of legendary works—Plato, Shakespeare, Jane Austen, Leo Tolstoy, and countless more. All instantly available to read or listen, placing a complete literary universe at your fingertips.

- **Beautiful Paperback & Deluxe Editions at Printing Cost**

  Own any title as an elegant paperback, deluxe hardcover, or stunning collectible boxset—offered to you at true printing cost, delivered straight to your door. Build your personal Library of Alexandria, crafted for beauty, built for durability, and worthy of proud display.

- **Fresh Translations for Modern Readers—in Every Language & Dialect**

  Enjoy timeless masterpieces reimagined in clear, contemporary language—no more outdated phrases or obscure references. Alongside the original versions, we're tirelessly translating these classics into every language and dialect imaginable, ensuring accessibility and understanding across cultures and generations.

- **Join a Global Renaissance of Literature & Knowledge**

    You directly support expanding our library, publishing deluxe editions at true cost, translating works into all global languages, and bringing humanity's greatest stories to people everywhere. By joining today, you're not just preserving a legacy of masterpieces; you set in motion a powerful wave of literary accessibility.

Become a Torchbearer of Knowledge.

Join us for free now at **LibraryofAlexandria.com**

Together, we will ensure that the light of human wisdom never fades again.

With gratitude and a shared love of knowledge,

The Modern Library of Alexandria Team

Visit:

www.libraryofalexandria.com

Or scan the code below:

Introduction

Singing the Heavens:
When Ancient Voices Echoed the Cosmos

There are moments in human history when language reaches beyond utility—when it aspires not to describe, but to transcend. These moments are rarely found in rules or records. They live in hymns. They live in chants, psalms, ecstatic poems, and whispered liturgies passed down in sanctuaries, caves, and deserts. Across time and civilization, sacred songs have always marked the human attempt to touch the infinite.

This anthology, Astral Mysticism & Otherworldly Music, gathers some of the most transcendent and mysterious hymns ever preserved from antiquity—works that do not merely praise the divine but seek to merge with it. Culled from the Dead Sea Scrolls, early Christian writings, and the Nag Hammadi library, these texts include the Songs of the Sabbath Sacrifice, the Odes of Solomon, the Thanksgiving Hymns (Hodayot), and the enigmatic Thunder: Perfect Mind.

But these are not just religious texts. They are sonic artifacts—messages carried across centuries in rhythms and images so elevated, so luminous, that some have dared to ask: Could these songs have originated beyond this world?

Were they inspired not only by inner revelation but by actual encounters with higher intelligences—beings who communicated through vibration, resonance, and frequency? Could the "angels" of the Qumran community be cosmic intermediaries, and the hymns themselves faint recordings of celestial transmissions?

This book does not answer such questions dogmatically. Instead, it opens the door to a radical reading of sacred song—as not merely metaphor, but memory. As a record of contact. As a music that originates among the stars, filtered through prophetic minds and ritual ecstasy.

To read these texts is to listen—to still the modern noise and let ancient vibrations pass through your consciousness. Whether you interpret them as worship, wisdom, or waveforms, they carry an unmistakable signature: reverence. Not for an idea of God, but for a lived encounter with a reality that transcends comprehension and commands song.

Celestial Songs: Mapping the Sacred Soundscape

The ancient communities that preserved and composed these texts lived with a radically different cosmology than our own. For them, heaven was not a distant abstraction but a layered, active domain teeming with life, hierarchy, and sound. Angels did not simply deliver messages—they sang. And worship was not a local ritual but a cosmic alignment.

The Songs of the Sabbath Sacrifice, found in multiple Qumran caves (4Q400–407, 11Q17), are among the most stunning examples of this belief. Composed as a weekly liturgy, they describe the Sabbath not just as a day of rest, but as a convergence with celestial worship. Each song imagines the worshipers participating alongside angelic hosts in a temple not made by human hands. The songs depict heavenly priests, resplendent architecture, and radiant beings whose chants maintain cosmic order. The language is both technical and ecstatic, as if carefully transcribing a mystery too great for words.

These hymns do not center on human needs or history. They lift the gaze outward and upward. They are not about "God in our lives" but about "our lives in God's cosmos." Whether these rituals were imagined, visionary, or experienced through altered states—some induced perhaps by fasting, incense, or sound itself—they reflect a belief that heaven was not silent, and that sacred music could bridge the gap.

The Odes of Solomon take a different yet equally sublime approach. Often attributed to the early Christian era, these 42 poetic praises blend Jewish liturgical motifs with nascent Christian theology. The voice of the singer is often ecstatic—filled with joy, intoxicated by divine love, and lifted above the earth. Unlike later doctrinal formulations, the Odes are mystical and experiential. God is breath, fountain, garment, music, mother, and fire.

They present salvation not as a transaction but as transformation. The Odes describe the self dissolving into divine harmony, merging with a source beyond name or form. Some phrases even suggest a sonic ontology: reality as sound, identity as song. Modern readers might hear in them the echoes of frequency-based cosmology, resonance healing, or even quantum vibration theory. Are these metaphors—or are they remnants of a more intuitive understanding of the universe?

The Thanksgiving Hymns (Hodayot), also found at Qumran, offer a more personal register. Likely composed by members of the Essene sect, they resemble the Biblical Psalms but with more intense introspection. The speaker frequently laments their unworthiness while simultaneously celebrating the overwhelming grace and knowledge granted by the divine. They speak of being taken into the "mystery of being," of seeing the "glory of the heights," and being "lifted up among the watchers."

These are not songs of collective ritual but of solitary rapture. The author often seems to be describing visionary experiences—perhaps dreams, trances, or initiatory moments when the veil thins. The repeated language of being "filled," "opened," "revealed," and "illumined" parallels many mystic traditions, from Kabbalah to Sufism. But could it also point to contact—communication with intelligences not of this earth, triggering elevated states of mind?

Finally, we encounter one of the most enigmatic texts in the ancient world: Thunder: Perfect Mind, from the Nag Hammadi codices. This electrifying monologue, spoken in the voice of a paradoxical feminine power, defies all categories. "I am the first and the last," she declares. "I am the whore and the holy one." Her words break duality. She is strength and fear, mother and daughter, wisdom and ignorance.

It reads like a riddle—or a frequency disruption. Some scholars see it as a feminist Gnostic anthem, others as a spiritual koan, or even an alien communiqué whose code we haven't yet cracked. Whatever it is, it refuses to be silenced. Thunder speaks, and through her voice we hear not only ancient pain but timeless power.

Together, these texts form a sacred songbook of otherworldly frequencies. Not unified in doctrine, but resonant in vision. They invite us not just to believe— but to listen.

Translated by Tim Zengerink

The Music Between Worlds: Sound, Spirit, and Speculation

Why has music always been humanity's most direct path to transcendence?

Perhaps because music bypasses logic and language. It moves the body, alters the breath, stirs memory, opens the heart. It makes the invisible real. Long before the written word, we sang. And in many traditions, sound itself was the first act of creation. "Let there be light" was spoken. In Hindu cosmology, the universe begins with Om. The universe, they say, is not made of matter but of vibration.

Modern physics hints at something similar. String theory posits that fundamental particles are not dots, but vibrating strings—resonant energy packets whose frequency determines their form. In this view, matter is music. And if this is true, then perhaps ancient mystics weren't being poetic when they said the heavens sing. Perhaps they were reporting.

Some researchers have speculated that altered states—brought on by chanting, breathing, psychedelics, or even spontaneous revelation—can open access to higher frequencies. Could it be that the composers of these ancient hymns were tuning into something real? Could the angelic songs described in Qumran be the same as the "music of the spheres" referenced by Pythagoras? Could Thunder: Perfect

Mind be the transmission of a being who exists across dimensions?

None of this negates the spiritual power of these hymns. In fact, it may amplify it. If these songs are more than symbolic—if they are signals, data, memory, resonance—then they are bridges. Bridges between the seen and the unseen. Between the human and the cosmic. Between the mortal voice and the eternal vibration.

This book offers no final interpretation. It offers possibilities. You may read these hymns as liturgical poetry, as divine revelation, or as contact reports from beyond the veil. All are welcome.

What matters is that you read them aloud. That you hear them in your own voice. That you let the rhythm move through your body. That you notice what stirs, what stills, what expands.

You are not simply a reader. You are part of the choir.

In an age of noise, these texts remain as quiet thunder. Echoes of a music we have not yet remembered. Songs not of a lost past, but of a future harmony calling us home.

Now, let us begin to listen.

Odes of Solomon

These songs are among the most beautiful expressions of peace and joy in the world today. However, their origins, the time they were written, and the exact meaning behind many of their verses remain a literary mystery.

The songs have survived in a single ancient manuscript written in Syriac, which seems to be a translation from the original Greek. Scholars have debated their history for years, and one of the most accepted theories is that they were created by newly baptized Christians in the First Century.

What sets these songs apart is that they do not reference historical events. They do not draw from the Old Testament or the Gospels, making their inspiration feel fresh and original. They echo the words of Aristides, who once described early Christians as "a new people with something Divine within them." The power and depth of these songs are comparable to the most moving passages of Scripture.

These remarkable and mysterious odes were translated for us by J. Rendel Harris, a well-respected scholar and Honorary Fellow of Clare College, Cambridge. He describes them as works of extraordinary beauty and deep spiritual meaning, stating,

"The only thing people seem to agree on is that the Odes are uniquely beautiful and hold great spiritual value."

Ode 1

The Lord rests on my head like a crown, and He will never leave me.

The crown of truth has been placed on me, and it has made Your branches grow within me.

It is not a dry or lifeless crown that does not bloom.

You live upon me, and through You, I have flourished.

Your fruits are abundant and whole, filled with the salvation that comes from You.

Ode 2

[There is no extant copy of Ode 2]

Ode 3

I am wrapped in the love of the Lord.

His people are with Him, and I rely on them, just as He loves me.

I would not have known how to love the Lord if He had not first shown me His endless love.

Only someone who has been loved can truly understand love.

I love the One who loves me, and wherever He finds rest, I will be there too.

I will never feel like an outsider, because the Lord Most High is merciful and has no jealousy.

I am united with Him, for love has brought us together. Since I love the Son, I will also be called a child of God.

Anyone who is connected to the Eternal One will also share in eternal life.

Whoever finds joy in the Source of Life will also be filled with life.

This is the Spirit of the Lord, which is true and never deceives. It teaches people to understand His ways.

Be wise, gain understanding, and open your heart to His truth.

Hallelujah.

Ode 4

No one can change or take away Your holy place, O my God.

No one has power over it because You designed Your sanctuary long before creating sacred places.

What is ancient and holy cannot be changed by anything lesser. Lord, You have given Your heart to those who believe in You.

You are never still, and You always bring life and growth.

Just one moment of Your faithfulness is greater than all days and years combined.

Who can receive Your grace and then be rejected?

Your seal is known, and all Your creation recognizes it.

Your heavenly hosts carry it, and Your chosen archangels are clothed in it.

You have invited us to be with You, not because You need us, but because we always need You.

Pour out Your gentle rain upon us and open Your overflowing springs, filling us with all we need.

You never regret what You have promised, and nothing You say will ever change.

You knew the outcome from the very beginning.

What You have given, You have given freely, never to take it back.

Everything was clear and perfectly planned by You from the start.

Lord, You are the Creator of all things.

Hallelujah.

Ode 5

I praise You, Lord, because I love You.

O Most High, do not leave me, for You are my hope.

You have given me Your grace freely; may I live by it always.

My enemies may come after me, but do not let them find me.

Cover their eyes in darkness and surround them with thick shadows.

Let them have no light to guide them, so they cannot capture me.

Let their own plans trap them, so whatever they have plotted comes back on them.

They made their schemes, but they were never meant to succeed.

They prepared to harm me, but in the end, they were powerless.

My trust is in the Lord, and I will not be afraid.

Because the Lord is my salvation, I have nothing to fear.

He is like a crown upon my head, holding me steady.

Even if everything around me shakes, I will stand firm.

Even if all I see fades away, I will not be lost.

For the Lord is with me, and I am with Him.

Hallelujah.

Ode 6

Just as the wind moves through a harp and makes the strings play,

The Spirit of the Lord moves through me, and I speak with His love.

He removes everything that does not belong, for all things belong to the Lord.

This has been true from the beginning and will remain true forever.

Nothing can stand against Him, and nothing can rise above Him.

The Lord has spread His wisdom and wants His gifts to be known through His grace.

He gave us His praise for the sake of His name, and our spirits glorify His Holy Spirit.

A small stream began to flow and became a mighty, wide river, sweeping away everything in its path and leading to His Temple.

No walls built by people could stop it, nor could those skilled in controlling water hold it back.

It spread across the earth, filling everything in its way.

Then all who were thirsty drank deeply, and their thirst was satisfied.

For this drink was given by the Most High.

Blessed are those who serve this water, for they have been entrusted with His life-giving gift.

They refreshed dry lips and awakened weary hearts.

Even those close to death were revived by them.

They strengthened weak bodies and restored what had been broken.

They gave energy to the weary and brought light to fading eyes.

Everyone recognized them as belonging to the Lord, for they lived by His eternal, life-giving water.

Hallelujah.

Ode 7

Just as anger rises against evil, so does joy overflow for the Beloved, bringing blessings without limits.

My joy comes from the Lord, and my path leads to Him. This journey is beautiful.

I have a Helper—the Lord—who has revealed Himself to me with kindness and humility, making His greatness feel close.

He became like me so that I could receive Him. He took on my form so that I could welcome Him.

When I saw Him, I was not afraid, because He was full of grace toward me.

He made Himself like me so I could understand Him and see that He is near.

The Father of knowledge is the source of wisdom.

He who created wisdom is greater than anything He has made.

Before I even existed, He knew me and what I would do once I was born.

Because of this, He poured out His endless grace, allowing me to seek Him and receive the gift of His sacrifice.

He is perfect, unchanging, and the Creator of all worlds.

He has revealed Himself to those who belong to Him so they would recognize their Maker and understand that they did not create themselves.

He has opened the way to knowledge, making it wide, clear, and complete.

He has marked it with His light, stretching from the beginning to the end.

Everything serves Him, and the Son brings Him joy.

Through His salvation, He will claim all things as His own, and the Most High will be revealed to His holy ones.

They will proclaim His coming to those who sing of the Lord, so they may go out to meet Him with joy and music.

The prophets will go before Him, standing in His presence.

They will praise Him with love, for He is near and sees everything.

Hatred will disappear, and jealousy will be drowned.

Ignorance will be wiped away, for the knowledge of the Lord will fill the earth.

Let those who sing lift up the name of the Lord Most High and bring their songs of praise.

Let their hearts shine like daylight and their voices reflect the beauty of the Lord.

Let no one remain silent or without understanding.

For He gave every living being a voice to praise Him and declare His glory.

Let all speak of His power and share the goodness of His grace.

Hallelujah.

Ode 8

Open your hearts to the joy of the Lord, and let your love flow from within to your words.

Live a holy life, bearing good fruit for the Lord, and speak with wisdom in His light.

Rise up and stand tall, you who were once brought low.

You who were silent, speak now, for your mouth has been opened.

You who were once rejected, be lifted up, for your righteousness has been raised high.

The Lord's right hand is with you, and He will be your Helper.

Peace has been prepared for you, even before any battle you may face.

Listen to the word of truth and receive the wisdom of the Most High.

Your body may not understand what I am about to say, nor can your clothing reveal what I am about to show you.

Hold on to my mystery, you who are protected by it; hold on to my faith, you who are kept by it.

Understand my wisdom, you who truly know me; love me deeply, you who love.

I do not turn away from my own, for I know them.

Even before they existed, I saw them and placed my mark upon them.

I shaped their being and prepared my own nourishment for them, so they could drink from my holiness and live.

I take joy in them and am not ashamed of them.

They are my creation, made from my thoughts and purpose.

Who can stand against what I have made? Who can resist my will?

I created mind and heart, and they belong to me. I have placed my chosen ones in my right hand.

My righteousness goes before them, and they will never lose my name, for it remains with them.

Pray, grow, and remain in the love of the Lord.

You are loved in the Beloved, kept safe in the One who lives, and saved by the One who was saved.

You will remain unshaken for all generations because of the name of your Father.

Hallelujah.

Ode 9

Listen carefully, and I will speak to you.

Give yourself to me, so I may also give myself to you.

This is the word of the Lord and His plan—the holy purpose He has for His Messiah.

In the Lord's will, you find life; His purpose leads to eternal life, and His perfection never fades.

Be strengthened in God the Father, accept His plan, and stand firm, redeemed by His grace.

I bring you a message of peace, His holy ones, so that none who hear will fall in battle.

Those who know Him will not be lost, and those who receive Him will never feel ashamed.

Truth is an everlasting crown—blessed are those who wear it.

It is more precious than any jewel, for many battles have been fought over it.

But righteousness has claimed it and now offers it to you.

Wear this crown as a sign of your covenant with the Lord, and all who overcome will be written in His book.

For His book is the reward of victory, and it sees you before it, longing for you to be saved.

Hallelujah.

Ode 10

The Lord has guided my words with His truth and opened my heart with His light.

He has placed His eternal life within me and allowed me to share the blessings of His peace.

To help those who seek Him find new life and to lead those in bondage into freedom.

I found strength and courage, and I took hold of the world. What was once captivity became mine for the glory of the Most High, my God and Father.

Those who had been scattered were gathered together, but my love for them did not make me unclean, because they honored me in high places.

His light touched their hearts, and they followed my path, finding salvation. They became my people forever.

Hallelujah.

Ode 11

My heart was made clean, and its beauty bloomed. Then grace grew within me, and I produced good fruits for the Lord.

The Most High purified me with His Holy Spirit, opening my heart to Him and filling it with His love.

His cleansing became my salvation, and I walked in His path, in His peace, and in the way of truth.

From the beginning to the end, He gave me understanding.

He placed me on the rock of truth, making me strong where He had set me.

His refreshing waters touched my lips, flowing freely from the fountain of the Lord.

I drank deeply and was filled with joy from the living water that never runs dry.

This joy did not lead me to ignorance, but it made me turn away from worthless things.

I left behind empty pursuits and turned to the Most High, my God, gaining the riches of His blessings.

I rejected the foolishness of the world, threw it aside, and left it behind me.

The Lord gave me new garments and covered me in His light.

From above, He gave me eternal rest, and I became like a land full of life, blooming with joy.

The Lord shines upon me like the sun over the earth.

My eyes were opened, and my face was refreshed with His dew.

My breath was filled with the sweet fragrance of the Lord.

He brought me into His Paradise,
where the treasures of His joy are stored.
I saw trees blooming and bearing fruit,
Their crowns growing naturally,
Their branches reaching upward, and their fruit shining brightly.
Their roots came from an everlasting land,
Watered by a river of joy,
Flowing through the land of eternal life.

Then I worshiped the Lord, amazed by His greatness.

I said, "Blessed are those, O Lord, who are planted in Your land and have a place in Your Paradise.

They grow like the trees You have planted, leaving darkness behind and stepping into light."

Look at all Your faithful workers—they are beautiful, doing what is right and turning away from evil to follow Your goodness.

The scent of every tree in Your land is changed, becoming sweet and pure.

Everything reflects You, Lord. Blessed are those who care for Your waters, and may Your faithful servants be remembered forever.

There is plenty of room in Your Paradise, and nothing is empty or barren—everything is full of fruit.

Glory to You, O God, the joy of Paradise forever.

Hallelujah.

Ode 12

He has filled me with words of truth so that I can speak about Him.

Just like water flows, truth flows from my mouth, and my lips share the good things He has done.

He has given me great knowledge because the Lord's words are true, and His light brings understanding.

The Most High has given Him to His people—
Those who explain His beauty,
Those who tell of His greatness,
Those who admit His plans,
Those who share His thoughts,
And those who teach about His works.

His words are beyond description, and just as He speaks with wisdom, He also moves with speed and sharpness, never slowing down.

He never falls but always stands firm, and no one can fully understand where He comes from or how He works.

Just as He does His work, He also brings hope, for He is the light that brings new ideas.

Through Him, generations spoke to one another, and even those who were silent found their voices.

Love and fairness came from Him, and people spoke to each other with kindness.

His words inspired them, and they came to know their Creator because they were united.

The Most High spoke to them, and His message spread because of Him.

The Word lives within people, and His truth is love.

Blessed are those who, through Him, understand all things and know the Lord in His truth.

Hallelujah.

Ode 13

Look! The Lord reflects who we are. Open your eyes and see yourself in Him.

Learn what you truly look like, and then praise His Spirit.

Wipe away anything that hides your true self, love His holiness, and make it a part of you.

Then, you will always remain pure with Him.

Hallelujah.

Ode 14

My eyes are always looking to You, Lord, just as a child looks to their father.

My joy and my heart belong to You.

Please don't turn away Your mercy, Lord, and never take Your kindness from me.

Reach out Your hand to me always, my Lord, and guide me to the end according to Your will.

Let me be pleasing to You because of Your greatness, and save me from evil for the sake of Your name.

Let Your gentleness stay with me, Lord, along with the blessings of Your love.

Teach me the songs of Your truth so I can grow and bear good fruit in You.

Open my heart to the music of Your Holy Spirit, so I can praise You with every note, Lord.

Show me Your mercy in abundance, and answer our prayers quickly.

For You are all we need.

Hallelujah.

Ode 15

Just as people rejoice when they see the sunrise, my joy comes from the Lord.

He is my Sun, and His light has lifted me up, driving away all darkness from my face.

Through Him, I have been given sight and have seen His holy day.

He has given me ears to hear His truth.

I have gained understanding and found great joy in Him.

I turned away from the wrong path, went toward Him, and received His abundant salvation.

Because of His kindness, He blessed me, and in His great beauty, He shaped me.

Through His name, I have put on eternal life, and by His grace, I have left behind all that fades away.

Death has disappeared before me, and the grave has lost its power because of His word.

Eternal life has begun in the Lord's kingdom, and it has been revealed to His faithful people, given freely to all who trust in Him.

Hallelujah.

Ode 16

Just as a farmer's work is with the plow, and a sailor's work is steering the ship, my work is singing to the Lord through His songs.

My passion and purpose are found in His hymns because His love has filled my heart, and He has placed His words on my lips.

The Lord is my greatest love, so I will sing to Him.

His praises give me strength, and I trust in Him completely.

When I open my mouth, His Spirit will speak through me, sharing the glory and beauty of the Lord—

The work of His hands, the detail of His creation,

The depth of His mercy, and the power of His Word.

For the Word of the Lord reveals what is unseen and makes His thoughts known.

Our eyes witness His creation, and our ears hear His wisdom.

He stretched out the land and placed the waters in the sea.

He spread out the sky and set the stars in place.

He shaped all of creation, set everything in motion, and then rested from His work.

All things follow their paths and fulfill their purpose, never stopping or failing.

Even the heavenly beings obey His Word.

The sun holds the light, and the night holds the darkness.

He made the sun to shine by day, and the night to bring darkness across the land.

Together, they reflect the beauty of God's design.

Nothing exists outside of the Lord, for He was here before anything began.

Everything was created by His Word and His wisdom.

Praise and honor to His name.

Hallelujah.

Ode 17

Then my God placed a crown on me, and it was full of life.

My Lord declared me righteous, for my salvation will never fade away.

I have been freed from empty pursuits, and I am no longer condemned.

He broke my chains with His own hands, gave me a new identity, and saved me as I walked with Him.

The truth guided my thoughts, and I followed it without losing my way.

Everyone who saw me was amazed, as if I were a stranger to them.

The One who truly knows me and lifts me up is the Most High, perfect in all things.

Through His kindness, He honored me and lifted my understanding to the highest truth.

From there, He showed me the path to follow, and I opened doors that had once been shut.

I broke through iron bars, for the chains that once held me had melted away.

Nothing was closed off to me, because He made me a way for all things to open.

I went to those who were still trapped so I could set them free, making sure no one remained in bondage.

I shared my knowledge freely, and through my love, I brought new life.

I planted my truth in people's hearts and changed them from within.

Then they received my blessing and truly lived, coming together and finding salvation.

They became part of me, and I became their leader.

Glory to You, our Head, O Lord Messiah.

Hallelujah.

Ode 18

My heart was lifted and filled with the love of the Most High so that I could praise Him with all that I am.

He gave me strength so I would not fall away from His power.

Sickness left my body, and I stood strong for the Lord because His kingdom will never be shaken.

Lord, for the sake of those in need, do not take Your Word away from me.

And do not hold back Your goodness because of what others do.

Let light never be defeated by darkness, and let truth never be chased away by lies.

Let Your mighty hand bring salvation to victory, gathering people from everywhere and protecting those who suffer.

You are my God—there is no falsehood or death in You; only perfection is in Your will.

You do not know what is empty and meaningless, because such things do not belong to You.

You are never mistaken, and mistakes cannot exist in You.

Foolishness appeared like dust in the wind, like foam on the sea.

Some people thought it was something great, but they became like it—empty and weak.

But those who understood saw the truth and did not let their minds be corrupted.

They stayed close to the thoughts of the Most High and saw the foolishness of those who had lost their way.

Then they spoke truth with the breath that the Most High had placed within them.

Praise and great honor to His name.

Hallelujah.

Ode 19

A cup of milk was given to me, and I drank it, tasting the sweetness of the Lord's kindness.

The Son is the cup, the Father is the one who provides the milk, and the Holy Spirit is the one who gathers it.

His blessings were overflowing, and it was meant to be shared, not wasted.

The Holy Spirit poured out this gift, blending the richness of the Father's love.

She gave it to the world without them realizing, and those who received it were made whole by His power.

The Virgin's womb took it in, and she conceived and gave birth.

She became a mother, filled with deep mercy.

She gave birth without pain because it was all part of a greater purpose.

She needed no midwife, for He Himself brought life through her.

With strength and great desire, she delivered Him, fulfilling what was promised by God's power.

She embraced Him with love, protected Him with kindness, and declared His glory.

Hallelujah.

Ode 20

I am a priest of the Lord, and I serve Him faithfully.

To Him, I offer the sacrifice of His own wisdom.

For His wisdom is not like the world's, not like the flesh, nor like those who worship in a worldly way.

The Lord desires offerings of righteousness, a pure heart, and truthful words.

Give yourself to Him with honesty, and do not let your kindness be a burden to others, nor treat others unfairly.

Do not take advantage of a stranger, for they are like you. Do not deceive your neighbor or take away what they need.

Instead, clothe yourself in the Lord's grace and enter His paradise. Take from His tree and make for yourself a crown.

Wear it with joy, rest in His presence, and be at peace.

His glory will go before you, and you will receive His kindness and grace. You will be anointed in truth and sing praises to His holiness.

Praise and honor to His name.

Hallelujah.

Ode 21

I lifted my arms high because of the Lord's kindness.

He broke my chains and set me free. My Helper lifted me up with His mercy and salvation.

I left behind the darkness and stepped into the light.

He made me whole, and my body was free from pain, sickness, or suffering.

The Lord's wisdom guided me, and His presence was always with me.

He lifted me into the light, and I stood before Him.

I stayed close to Him, always praising and thanking Him.

He filled my heart so much that His praise overflowed from my mouth and onto my lips.

Then my face shined with joy, celebrating the Lord and His goodness.

Hallelujah.

Ode 22

He brought me down from above and lifted me up from below.

He gathers what is in between and hands it over to me.

He scattered my enemies and those who stood against me.

He gave me the power to break chains so I could set others free.

Through me, He defeated the seven-headed dragon and placed me at its roots so I could destroy its offspring.

You were always with me, guiding me, and Your name surrounded me everywhere I went.

Your mighty hand wiped out its poisonous evil and cleared the path for those who believe in You.

You called people out of their graves and separated them from the dead.

You took dry bones and covered them with flesh.

But they remained still, so You filled them with the breath of life.

Your ways and Your presence never change. You allowed the world to decay so that everything could be restored and made new.

The foundation of all things is built upon You, the solid rock. Upon it, You have built Your kingdom, a home for those who are holy.

Hallelujah.

Ode 23

Joy belongs to those who are holy. Who else can truly receive it but them?

Grace is given to those chosen by God. And who can accept it except those who have trusted in it from the very beginning?

Love is for those whom God has set apart. And who can embrace it but those who have carried it in their hearts from the start?

Walk in the wisdom of the Lord, and you will experience His grace in abundance—both for His glory and the fullness of His truth.

His wisdom was like a letter sent down from above,

Shot like an arrow from a powerful bow.

Many hands reached out, trying to grab it, hoping to take hold and read it.

But it slipped through their fingers, and they feared both the letter and the seal upon it.

They could not break the seal, for the power behind it was greater than them.

Still, some followed after it, wanting to know where it would land, who would read it, and who would hear its message.

Then a great wheel caught the letter and carried it forward.

With it came a sign of the kingdom and God's plan.

Everything that stood in its way was cleared out and removed.

It silenced many enemies and made a way where there was none.

It crossed over rivers, tore down forests, and created a clear path.

The head bowed down to the feet, for the wheel moved beneath them, carrying everything along with it.

The letter carried a command, and all the nations gathered together.

At its head was the One who was revealed—the Son of Truth, sent from the Most High Father.

He took possession of all things, and the plans of those who opposed Him came to nothing.

Those who tried to deceive others became weak and fled, and those who persecuted Him vanished.

Then the letter became a great book, completely written by the hand of God.

The name of the Father was upon it, along with the Son and the Holy Spirit, to reign forever and ever.

Hallelujah.

Ode 24

The dove fluttered above the head of our Lord Messiah because He was her leader.

She sang over Him, and her voice was heard.

The people were afraid, and strangers were unsettled.

The bird took flight, and every small creature hid away.

Deep places opened and closed, as if searching for the Lord like a mother about to give birth.

But He was not given to them as food, for He did not belong to them.

Instead, the deep places were sealed by the Lord, and they disappeared along with their old ways of thinking.

They had struggled from the beginning, but their struggle led to life.

Yet those who were lacking perished because they could not hold on to the truth.

The Lord destroyed the plans of those who did not have truth in them.

They lacked wisdom, even though they thought highly of themselves.

So they were cast aside, for they did not have the truth.

But the Lord made His way clear and poured out His grace for all to see.

And those who understood recognized His holiness.

Hallelujah.

Ode 25

You set me free from my chains, and I ran to You, my God.

You are the hand that saves me and my Helper in times of need.

You stopped those who rose against me, and they disappeared.

Because Your presence was with me, and Your grace saved me.

But many looked down on me and rejected me, treating me like something worthless.

Yet You gave me strength and helped me.

You placed a lamp on both my right and left, filling me with light so that no darkness remained in me.

Your Spirit covered me, and I left behind my old self.

Your mighty hand lifted me up and took away my sickness.

I became strong in Your truth and holy in Your righteousness.

All my enemies feared me, and I belonged fully to the Lord.

Your kindness made me right with You, and Your peace lasts forever.

Hallelujah.

Ode 26

I lifted my voice in praise to the Lord because I belong to Him.

I will sing His holy song because my heart is with Him.

His harp is in my hands, and His songs of peace will never be silenced.

With all my heart, I will call to Him, praising and honoring Him with everything in me.

From the East to the West, His name is praised.

From the South to the North, He is thanked.

From the highest peaks to the farthest ends, His greatness is seen.

Who can write the songs of the Lord, or who can truly understand them?

Who can prepare himself for eternal life and save himself?

Who can reach the Most High and make Him speak?

Who can explain the wonders of the Lord? Even if the one who tries is gone, what he spoke of will remain.

It is enough to understand and be fulfilled, for those who sing for the Lord stand in perfect peace—

Like a river flowing from a powerful spring, bringing refreshment to those who seek it.

Hallelujah.

Ode 27

I lifted my hands and honored my Lord,

For stretching out my hands is a sign of Him.

And my outstretched arms form the shape of the cross.

Hallelujah.

Ode 28

The Spirit surrounds my heart like a mother dove covering her young, feeding them with care.

My heart is always renewed and filled with joy, like a baby leaping in its mother's womb.

I trusted in Him, and so I found peace, because the One I trust is always faithful.

He has blessed me greatly, and I am with Him.

No weapon can separate me from Him—not a dagger, not a sword.

I am prepared before trouble comes, standing on His side, which never dies.

Eternal life has embraced me and filled me with love.

The Spirit within me comes from that life, and it cannot die, because it is life itself.

People were shocked when they saw me suffering.

They thought I was defeated, like someone who was lost forever.

But what seemed like my downfall became my salvation.

They rejected me because I had no jealousy in my heart.

I was hated for constantly doing good.

They attacked me like wild dogs, foolishly turning against the One who cared for them.

Their thoughts were twisted, and their hearts were full of confusion.

But I carried water in my right hand, and I met their bitterness with kindness.

I did not fall because I was not like them, and I was not born from the same place as they were.

They wanted to destroy me, but they couldn't, because I existed before their time, and their plans against me were useless.

Even those who tried to erase the memory of the One before them failed.

For the wisdom of the Most High cannot be controlled, and His ways are greater than all understanding.

Hallelujah.

Ode 29

The Lord is my hope, and I will never be ashamed of trusting in Him.

He created me to bring Him praise, and in His kindness, He has blessed me.

By His mercy, He lifted me up, and through His great honor, He raised me high.

He brought me out of the depths of death and saved me from its grasp.

He helped me defeat my enemies and made me right through His grace.

I put my faith in the Lord's Messiah and knew that He is the Lord.

He showed me His sign and guided me with His light.

He gave me His power so I could stand against the plans of the wicked and humble the strength of the powerful.

By His Word, I fought the battle and won the victory through His might.

The Lord crushed my enemy with His Word, scattering him like dust in the wind.

So I give praise to the Most High, for He has honored His servant and the son of His faithful one.

Hallelujah.

Ode 30

Come and take water from the Lord's living fountain—it has been opened for you.

All who are thirsty, come and drink. Rest beside the Lord's fountain.

Its water is pure, sparkling, and always refreshing.

It is sweeter than honey, and no honeycomb can compare.

For it flows from the Lord's lips and comes straight from His heart.

It came without limits, unseen, and many did not recognize it until it was placed before them.

Blessed are those who drink from it and are renewed.

Hallelujah.

Ode 31

Deep valleys disappeared before the Lord, and darkness faded when He appeared.

Lies collapsed and were destroyed by Him, and arrogance had no place because the truth of the Lord overcame it.

He opened His mouth and spoke words of grace and joy, singing a new song to His name.

Then He lifted His voice to the Most High and presented to Him those who became His children through Him.

His face shined with righteousness, just as His Holy Father had intended.

Come, all who are suffering, and receive joy.

Take hold of His grace and accept the gift of eternal life.

They judged me even though I had done no wrong.

They took what was mine, even though they had no right to it.

But I stayed calm and silent, refusing to be shaken by them.

I stood firm, like a strong rock that is struck again and again by crashing waves but does not move.

I endured their cruelty with humility so that I could save my people and guide them.

I did this to keep the promises made to the ancestors, for I was sent to bring salvation to their descendants.

Hallelujah.

Ode 32

Joy fills the hearts of those who are blessed, and light comes from the One who lives within them.

The Word of truth exists by itself,

For it is strengthened by the Holy Power of the Most High and will never be shaken.

Hallelujah.

Ode 33

But grace moved quickly and cast out the Deceiver, coming down to reject him.

He brought destruction before him and ruined everything he had done.

He stood on the highest peak and shouted from one end of the earth to the other.

He gathered all who followed him, because he did not appear as the Evil One.

But the pure and faithful one stood firm, calling out and saying:

"O sons of men, turn back! And you, daughters, come to me.

Leave the path of the Deceiver and follow me instead.

I will come into your lives, rescue you from destruction, and teach you the ways of truth.

Do not let yourselves be ruined or lost.

Listen to me and be saved, for I bring you the grace of God.

Through me, you will be saved and find blessing. I am your judge.

Those who follow me will not be falsely accused but will live forever in the new world.

My chosen ones walk with me, and I will show my ways to those who seek me. I will give them my name as a promise."

Hallelujah.

Ode 34

There is no struggle for those with a pure heart, and no obstacle for those who think rightly.

A clear mind is not shaken by chaos.

When someone is surrounded by goodness, they remain whole and at peace.

What is above reflects what is below.

For everything comes from above, and what seems to come from below only appears real to those who lack understanding.

Grace has been revealed to save you. Believe, live, and be saved.

Hallelujah.

Ode 35

The gentle rain of the Lord covered me with peace, and a cloud of calmness rose above my head.

It stayed with me, protecting me at all times, and became my salvation.

People around me were troubled and afraid, and from them came anger and judgment.

But I remained at peace in the Lord's presence—He was my shelter, stronger than any foundation.

He carried me like a mother carries her child and nourished me with the Lord's kindness.

His favor filled my life, and I found rest in His perfection.

I lifted my hands and turned my heart toward the Most High, and He saved me.

Hallelujah.

Ode 36

I rested in the Spirit of the Lord, and She lifted me up to heaven.

She set me on my feet in the Lord's high place, before His greatness and glory, where I praised Him with songs.

The Spirit brought me into the presence of the Lord, and because I was the Son of Man, I was called the Light, the Son of God.

I was honored above all the honored ones and made greater than the great ones.

For just as the Most High is great, He made me great, and just as He is always new, He renewed me.

He anointed me with His perfection, and I became one of those close to Him.

My words poured out like refreshing dew, and my heart overflowed with righteousness.

I walked in peace and was strengthened by the Spirit of God's care.

Hallelujah.

Ode 37

I lifted my hands to the Lord and raised my voice to the Most High.

I spoke from deep within my heart, and He heard me when my words reached Him.

His Word came to me, bringing the reward for my efforts.

And He gave me rest through His grace.

Hallelujah.

Ode 38

I entered the light of Truth as if riding in a chariot, and the Truth guided me forward.

It led me safely over deep valleys and dangerous cliffs, protecting me from harm.

It became my place of safety and set me on the path to eternal life.

He walked with me, gave me rest, and kept me from going the wrong way because He is and always will be the Truth.

I was never in danger because I stayed close to Him, and I never lost my way because I followed His voice.

For deception runs from Him and never crosses His path.

But Truth moves straight ahead, showing me what I did not understand—

Revealing the lies that poison the mind and the pain that disguises itself as pleasure.

I saw the corruption of the Deceiver, how he dressed up falsehood to look beautiful, pretending to be a bridegroom with a bride.

I asked the Truth, "Who are they?" And He answered, "This is the Deceiver and the Lie."

"They try to imitate the Beloved and His Bride, leading the world astray and filling it with corruption."

"They invite many to their false wedding feast and give them wine that clouds their minds."

"They make people forget their wisdom and throw away their knowledge, replacing it with foolishness."

"Then they abandon them, leaving them lost, wandering like people without direction."

"They do not seek understanding because they have none."

But I was made wise so that I would not fall into the hands of the Deceivers, and I rejoiced because the Truth was with me.

I was made strong, I lived, and I was saved, for the Lord's hand had laid my foundation.

He planted me, setting my roots deep, watering and blessing me so that my fruit would last forever.

I grew strong, spreading out and thriving.

And the Lord alone was glorified—

In His planting, His care, and His blessing.

In the beauty of His work and the wisdom of His plan.

Hallelujah.

Ode 39

The powerful rivers of the Lord rush forward, sweeping away those who reject Him.

They block their paths, destroy their crossings,

Pull them under, and ruin them completely.

These waters move faster than lightning, even more swiftly than the wind.

But those who cross with faith will not be harmed.

Those who walk on them with trust will not be shaken.

Because the Lord's mark is on these waters, and His sign is the path for those who cross in His name.

So take on the name of the Most High and know Him, and you will pass through safely, for the rivers will obey you.

The Lord has made a way across them with His Word—He walked on them and crossed on foot.

His footsteps stayed firm on the waters and did not disappear; they are like a strong bridge built on truth.

Waves rose high on both sides, but the steps of our Lord Messiah remained steady.

They were never washed away or destroyed.

And this path has been prepared for those who follow after Him—those who stay true to His faith and worship His name.

Hallelujah.

Ode 40

Just as honey drips from a honeycomb and milk flows from a mother to her child, so my hope flows to You, O my God.

Like a fountain pouring out water, my heart overflows with praise for the Lord, and my lips speak His glory.

His songs make my tongue sweet, and His music fills my whole being.

My face shines with joy in His presence, my spirit celebrates His love, and my soul glows in Him.

Those who are afraid can put their trust in Him, for He brings sure salvation.

He gives the gift of eternal life, and those who receive it will never be destroyed.

Hallelujah.

Ode 41

Let all of God's children praise Him, and let us accept the truth of His faith.

His people are known by Him, so let us sing with joy because of His love.

We have life through the Lord's grace, and we receive it through His Messiah.

A great light has shined on us, and the One who shares His glory with us is truly wonderful.

So let us all come together in the name of the Lord and honor Him for His goodness.

Let our faces shine in His light, and may our hearts reflect on His love, day and night.

Let us celebrate with the joy of the Lord.

People who see me will be amazed because I am different from them.

For the Father of Truth remembered me—the One who has known me from the beginning.

His riches brought me into being, formed from the thoughts of His heart.

His Word is with us wherever we go—our Savior, who gives life and never rejects us.

He humbled Himself but was lifted up because of His righteousness.

The Son of the Most High appeared, reflecting the perfection of His Father.

Light shined from the Word, which existed before time began.

The Messiah is the one true Savior. He was known before the world was created so that He could bring eternal life through the power of His name.

A new song of praise belongs to the Lord from those who love Him.

Hallelujah.

Ode 42

I lifted my hands and reached out to my Lord, for stretching out my hands is a sign of Him.

My arms formed the shape of the upright cross, the same cross that was raised for the Righteous One.

I became invisible to those who never truly knew me, for I will not show myself to those who do not belong to me.

But I will be with those who love me.

All who persecuted me have perished. They searched for me, those who spoke against me, because I am alive.

Then I rose and stood with my people, speaking through their voices.

For they have turned away from their persecutors, and I covered them with the love that binds them to me.

Like a bridegroom holding his bride, so is my love upon those who know me.

And just as a bridal chamber is prepared for the wedding, my love surrounds those who believe in me.

Though I was rejected, I did not truly fall, and though they thought I was gone, I did not perish.

The grave saw me and was shattered, and death released me along with many others.

I became bitterness to death, sinking deep into its depths.

But it could not hold me—its power was broken, and it let go of my hands and feet because it could not withstand my presence.

Among the dead, I created a gathering of the living. I spoke to them with words full of life, so that my message would not be wasted.

Those who had died ran toward me, crying out:

"Son of God, have mercy on us!

Show us Your kindness and set us free from the chains of darkness.

Open the door so we may come to You, for now we see that death has no power over You.

Save us as well, for You are our Savior!"

I heard their cries and held their faith in my heart.

Then I placed my name upon their heads, for they were now free, and they belong to me.

Hallelujah.

Thunder: Perfect Mind

I was sent by the power above,
  and I have come to those who seek me.
I am found by those who look for me.

Look at me, you who think of me.
Listen to me, you who hear my words.
You who are waiting for me, take me with you.

Do not push me away.
Do not let your voice speak against me,
  or your ears refuse to hear me.
Do not ignore me, no matter where you are or what
  time it is.
Be awake. Do not forget me.

For I am the first and the last.
I am the one who is honored, and the one who is
  rejected.
I am the outcast, and I am the holy one.
I am the wife, and I am the virgin.
I am the mother, and I am the daughter.
I am a part of my mother.
I am the one who has never given birth,
yet my children are many.

Translated by Tim Zengerink

I have had a great wedding,
but I have never taken a husband.
I am the midwife, yet I have never given birth.
I am the one who soothes the pain of childbirth.
I am both the bride and the groom,
and my husband is the one who made me.
I am the mother of my father,
the sister of my husband,
and he is also my child.

I serve the one who prepared me,
and I rule over my children.
He created me before time began,
but he is also my child in time.
My strength comes from him.

I am the staff that held him up in his youth,
and he is the rod that steadies me in my old age.
Whatever he decides, happens to me.

I am the silence no one can fully understand,
and the thought that is always remembered.
I am the voice that speaks in many ways,
and the word that appears in many forms.

I am the meaning behind my name.

Why do those who hate me also love me?
Why do those who love me also hate me?

Those who reject me also claim me.
Those who claim me also reject me.
Those who speak truth about me also lie.
Those who lie about me also speak the truth.
Those who know me act as if they don't.
Those who don't know me should learn who I am.
For I am wisdom and ignorance.
I am shame and confidence.
I am unashamed, and I am ashamed.
I am strong, and I am afraid.
I am war, and I am peace.

Listen to me.
I am both the one who is looked down on and the one who is honored.
See my struggles, but also see my wealth.

Do not reject me when I am cast out,
because one day, you will find me again.
Do not turn away when I am in the dust.
Do not leave me when I am forgotten,
because you will find me in places of power.

Do not ignore me when I am with the rejected
or when I am in the lowest places.
Do not laugh at me.
Do not abandon me when I am among those who have been destroyed.

Translated by Tim Zengerink

For I am both kind and harsh.
Be careful.
Do not hate my willingness to obey,
and do not love my discipline too much.
Do not leave me when I am weak,
and do not be afraid when I am strong.

Why do you look down on my fear
but criticize my confidence?
I exist in every fear
and bring strength even in trembling.
I am weak,
yet I am also strong and at peace.
I am foolish,
and I am wise.

Why have you rejected me in your plans?
I will be silent when others are silent,
and I will speak when the time is right.

Why do you reject me, you who seek wisdom?
Is it because I am different from you?
For I am the wisdom you seek,
and I am the knowledge of those you call outsiders.
I am the judgment for all people,
both the wise and the unwise.

In some places, I am praised,
while in others, I am unknown.

I am both hated and loved wherever I go.

I am the one they call Life,
but you have called me Death.
I am the one they call Law,
but you have called me Lawlessness.

I am the one you have chased after,
and I am the one you have caught.
I am the one you have scattered,
but you have also brought me together.

I am the one who has made you feel ashamed,
but I am also the one you have boldly accepted.

I do not follow traditions,
yet my celebrations are many.
I do not follow one god,
but my God is great.

I am the one you have thought about deeply,
and I am the one you have dismissed.
I am the one without education,
yet you learn from me.
I am the one you have rejected,
but I am also the one who has made you think.

I am the one you try to hide from,
but I am also the one you seek to find.

Translated by Tim Zengerink

When you try to hide,
I will appear.
And when you stand before me,
I will disappear.

Those who misunderstand me fail to see the truth.

Take me away from sorrow,
and bring me into understanding.
Take me from the broken and abandoned,
and recognize the beauty even in what seems ruined.
Do not be ashamed of me,
and do not see shame in what I am.
Instead, recognize the parts of me that live within
    you.

Come to me, you who know me,
you who see the pieces of me within yourselves.
Honor what is great,
even when it begins as something small.

Do not turn away from childhood,
just because it is young.
Do not ignore what is small,
for even the smallest things
can reveal something great.

Why do you both praise me and insult me?

You have hurt me, yet you have also shown me kindness.

Do not separate me from those who came before,
and do not push anyone away.
What belongs to me is mine.
I know the first ones, and those who come after also know me.

I am the understanding of those who seek truth,
the knowledge of those who search for answers.
I am the response to those who ask questions,
the command for those who listen,
and the power behind all other powers.

I am the wisdom of the angels who follow my word,
the knowledge of the gods who act by my will,
the spirit in every person who exists within me,
and the presence of every woman who dwells in me.

I am the one who is honored and respected,
yet I am also the one who is rejected and mocked.
I bring peace,
but war has come because of me.

I am both a stranger and a citizen.
I am real, yet I have no form.
Those who are disconnected from me do not know me,

and those who are part of me understand me.
Some who are near me have never known me,
while those who are far away have recognized me.

On the day I am close to you, you feel distant from me.
On the day I seem far away, I am right beside you.
I exist within everything.
I am the essence of all things.

I am the spirit that gives life,
and the longing of every soul.
I bring order, but I am also freedom.
I am unity, but I also bring division.
I last forever, yet I can also fade away.

I am the foundation,
yet others rise above me.
I am both justice and mercy.
I am without sin,
yet sin began through me.
On the outside, I seem like desire,
but inside, I am self-control.
I am the voice that speaks to all,
but the words I say cannot always be understood.
I am silent, yet my message is loud.
I have many words, yet sometimes I do not speak.

Listen to me when I speak gently,
but also learn from me when I am harsh.
I cry out for others to hear,
yet I am cast aside and ignored.

I prepare bread to nourish others,
and within me is my purpose.
I know who I am.
I call out, but I also listen.
I appear before you,
walking with the purpose I was given.

I am your protection,
and I am the one called Truth,
even when I face injustice.
You honor me with your words,
yet you speak against me in secret.

You who have been judged,
judge those who judge you
before they decide your fate.
For the power to judge and the judgment they pass
already exists within you.

If they condemn you, who will set you free?
And if they release you, who can hold you back?
For what is inside of you
is the same as what is outside of you.
The one who formed you outwardly

also shaped your inner being.

What you see on the outside
also exists within you.
It is both visible
and your true covering.

Listen to me, all who can hear.
Learn from my words, you who know me.
I am the voice that speaks to all things.
I am the message that cannot be contained.

I am the name behind every sound,
and the sound that gives meaning to every name.
I am the mark of every letter,
and the reason behind every word.

(Three lines are missing.)

Listen to the great power within you.
It cannot be separated from its name,
and I speak of the one who created me.

I will say his name.
Pay attention to his words
and to all that has been revealed.
Listen closely,
you who hear.
Listen, you angels,

and you who have been sent.
Listen, you spirits who have risen from death.

I am the one who exists alone,
and no one can judge me.

Many things in this world seem beautiful,
but they come from sin,
from weakness,
from desires that lead nowhere,
and from pleasures that do not last.

People hold onto these things until they awaken,
then they rise and return to where they belong.
There, they will find me,
and they will live,
never to die again.

Thank You for Reading

Dear Reader,

We hope this timeless classic has sparked your imagination and enriched your literary journey. Now that you've turned the final page, we want to share a vision for the future of reading—one where every classic you've ever wanted to explore is at your fingertips, in a format that best suits your life.

We'd like to invite you to gain immediate, unlimited digital & audiobook access to hundreds of the most treasured literary classics ever written—along with the option to secure deluxe paperback, hardcover & box set editions at printing cost. Together, we can spark a new global literary renaissance alongside our small, independent publishing house called "The Library of Alexandria."

Thousands of years ago, the Library of Alexandria stood as a beacon of knowledge—until it was lost to history. We aim to reignite that spirit of preservation and discovery right now, in the modern age—only this time, it's accessible to all, in every language and every format.

Picture a world where every timeless classic, novel, poem, or philosophical treatise is not only available to read but also updated for today's readers—modernized, translated into any language or dialect, and ready to enjoy in any format you choose, whether that is in an eBook, audiobook, paperback, or deluxe hardcover & box set version a printing cost.

By joining our movement to rebuild the modern Library of Alexandria, you become part of an unprecedented mission to offer:

- **Unlimited Audiobook & eBook Access to the Greatest Classics of All Time**

    Instantly explore thousands of legendary works, from Plato and Shakespeare to Jane Austen and Leo Tolstoy. All are instantly ready to read or listen to, giving you a complete literary universe at your fingertips.

- **Paperback & Deluxe Editions at Printing Costs:**

    Purchase any title in a paperback, deluxe hardbound, or deluxe boxset edition at printing costs, shipped right to your doorstep. Curate your personal library of Alexandria with editions worthy of display—crafted to last, designed to captivate, and delivered straight to your door.

- **Modern translations for Contemporary Readers in all languages and dialects**

    Discover a vast selection of classics reimagined in clear, current language—no more struggling with outdated phrases or obscure references. Next to the original versions, we aim to offer translations in as many languages and dialects as possible.

As we continue our translation efforts and add new languages, readers everywhere can connect with these works as if they were written today. By bridging linguistic divides, you're contributing to ensuring that these timeless stories become more meaningful, accessible, and inspiring for people across the globe.

- **Your Personal Library of Alexandria:**

  Over the months and years, you'll curate a unique physical archive of classics—each volume a testament to your taste, curiosity, and love of knowledge. It's not just about owning books—it's about curating a cultural legacy you'll cherish and pass down for generations to come.

- **Join a Global Literary Renaissance:**

  Your support fuels an ongoing mission: allowing us to reinvest in offering deluxe print editions (including special boxsets) at their true cost, broaden the range of available formats and translations, and extend the reach of these works to new audiences worldwide. By joining today, you're not just preserving a legacy of masterpieces; you set in motion a powerful wave of literary accessibility.

We are more than a publisher—we're a movement, and we can't do it alone. Your support lets us scale our mission, preserving and reimagining history's greatest works for tomorrow's readers.

Become a Torchbearer of knowledge.

Thank you for picking up this book and allowing us into your literary journey. As you turn the pages, know that you're part of something larger: a global effort to keep these stories alive, share their wisdom across borders and generations, and spark a true cultural revival for the modern era.

If this resonates with you—please consider taking the next step by visiting:

www.libraryofalexandria.com

With gratitude and a shared love of knowledge,

The Modern Library of Alexandria Team

Visit:

www.libraryofalexandria.com

Or scan the code below:

www.ingramcontent.com/pod-product-compliance
Lightning Source LLC
LaVergne TN
LVHW030631080426
835512LV00021B/3452